Cherish each Moment!
Karen Slocum

Kimberly,
    thanks for filling my life
with pride, joy, and love.
    Enjoy this book it's outstanding—
                Love,
                Mom
                8/21/01

This book is a
gift in honor of

_____, an

extraordinary mom.

With love

from_____

Date_____

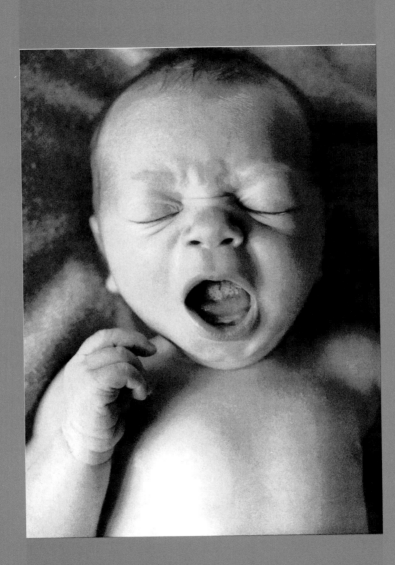

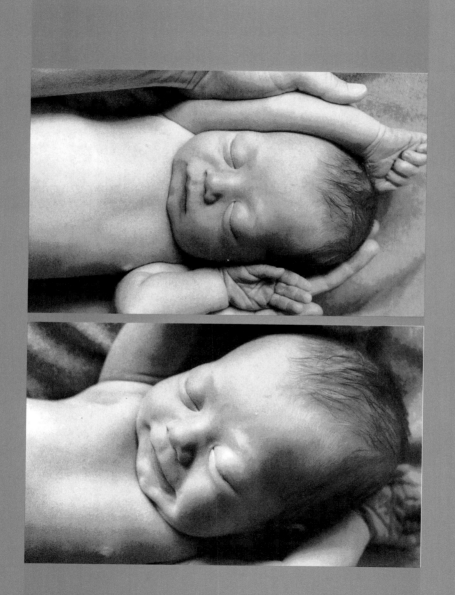

No Greater Love

No Greater Love

Being
an Extraordinary
Mom

Loren Slocum

ST. MARTIN'S PRESS
NEW YORK

Designed by Gwen Petruska Gürkan
Page layout by MM Design 2000, Inc.

Library of Congress Cataloging-in-Publication Data

Slocum, Loren.
      No greater love: being an extraordinary mom / Loren Slocum.
         p.   cm.
     ISBN 1–58238–056–2 (alk. paper)
      1. Motherhood.   2. Mother and infant.   3. Mother and child.
   I. Title
   HQ759.S58   1999   99–15407
   306.874'3—DC21

First edition: October 1999

10 9 8 7 6 5 4 3 2 1

*B*EFORE YOU WERE CONCEIVED
I WANTED YOU
BEFORE YOU WERE BORN
I LOVED YOU
BEFORE YOU WERE AN HOUR OLD
I WOULD DIE FOR YOU
THIS IS THE MIRACLE OF LOVE

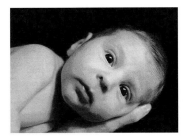

—*Maureen Hawkins*

ACKNOWLEDGMENTS

This book is dedicated to all those who have reminded me that I am extremely blessed.

My parents, Arlene and Joseph Schandler, who have always instilled in me that anything is possible with the power of love and sincere intent. For always cheering me on (even when I know sometimes they didn't know what they were cheering for). My mother, a woman full of life, who makes every moment an adventure, most of all for giving me the insight to trust my creative spirit. My father, for being a living example of God in my life and in the lives of those who have the good fortune to cross his path. For being the kindest, most patient, and most sincere man I have ever met.

Shore, for being my number one raving fan and my best friend. For his reservoir of creativity. For truly believing in my vision, my unique talents, and most of all for believing in the essence of who I am. Finally, for being patient with me and seeking to understand the way I am feeling.

My son, Josua, for reminding me what life is about. For being my greatest teacher and a pure example of unconditional love. For bringing more joy, laughter, and love into my life than I ever thought possible.

My brother, David, for being a constant and solid foundation in my family, whom I feel so lucky to have as my big brother.

God, for blessing me with the gift of motherhood, and a chance to play and learn from all the experiences in this life. For the little voice I call intuition, which—when I listen to it—always leads me in the right direction.

Colleen Futch Morgans for having such a gifted eye that captures the essence of what this book is about.

Kelly Giezentanner for her gifted eye.

Shannon McCann and Paige Nussbaumer, who seem to know what I am saying, even when I'm not talking.

Laura Yorke, Editor at Large of Golden Books, for being a walking example of "An Extraordinary Mother." For her creativity and dedication to this book.

Lara Asher, associate editor at St. Martin's, for her love, committment, and passion for this book.

Jan Miller and her staff at Dupree Miller for guiding me on the path to make this dream a reality.

To the family that I was fortunate enough to become a part of. I have felt so welcome, loved, and supported by you all . . . Heidi, Nancie, Barc, TD, Clay, Wendy, Katie, and R. C. (in his memory).

Heidi Krupp—A woman full of laughter, spirit, and tenacious energy who never takes no for an answer, and has the unique ability to always make me feel special.

Mrs. Ross—My fifth grade English teacher, and Herb the Verb!

Onisha, Shareena, Sawkia, Comara, and Juanita—"My Girls"—for being my inspirations that lit the candle of desire for me to be a mother. Because of all the magic moments we shared together.

To my chosen family, who are not blood family but whom I consider as real as any family I have. They challenge me to be my best, they give me a place to escape the craziness of the world. They are my mentors, sounding boards, guidance counselors, and much more. In one thing I am certain: that whatever I need I can always find within these hearts, minds, and souls . . . Tani, Jayne, Tina, Joelle, Eric, Jackson, Albert, Brooks, Ann, Vickie, Gail, Kirstin, Brian, Emily, Carolyn, Mary, Michele, Paula, Kathy, Sam, Lynn, Sissy, Wendy, Wendy D., Kathy B., Joseph, Deb, Alice, Chris, Alissa, Maya, Monique, Stan, Mandy, Baby Jack, Gary, Pam, John, Sarah, Jennifer, Brannon, Kim, Joe, William, Vicki, Diana, Joe, Libby, Liz, Sue, EB, Melanie, and the entire Crew and Trainer teams of the Anthony Robbins Companies Events.

I have extracted my question process from the work of a good friend—a man I am indebted to, who has dramatically changed the lives of many people around the world—Anthony Robbins. His wife, Becky, a truly inspiring woman, dynamic businessperson, and amazing mom, also deserves acknowledgment for the example she has set as a mother and for living the principles that I share in this book.

Each of you will always be a part of me.

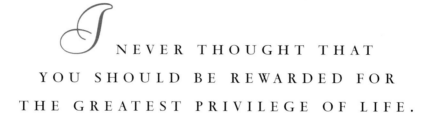

I NEVER THOUGHT THAT
YOU SHOULD BE REWARDED FOR
THE GREATEST PRIVILEGE OF LIFE.

—*Mary Roper Coker,*
on being chosen Mother of the Year 1958

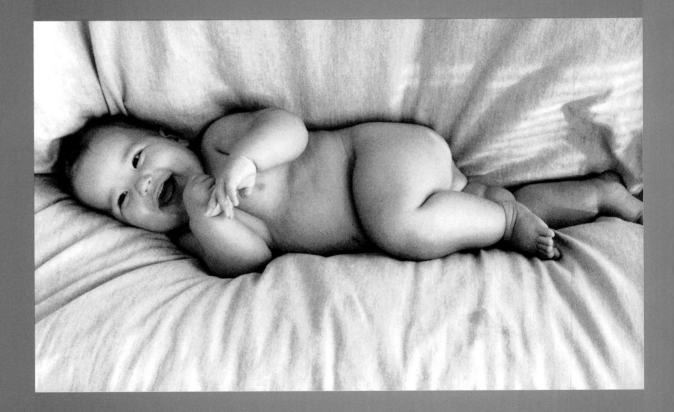

CONTENTS

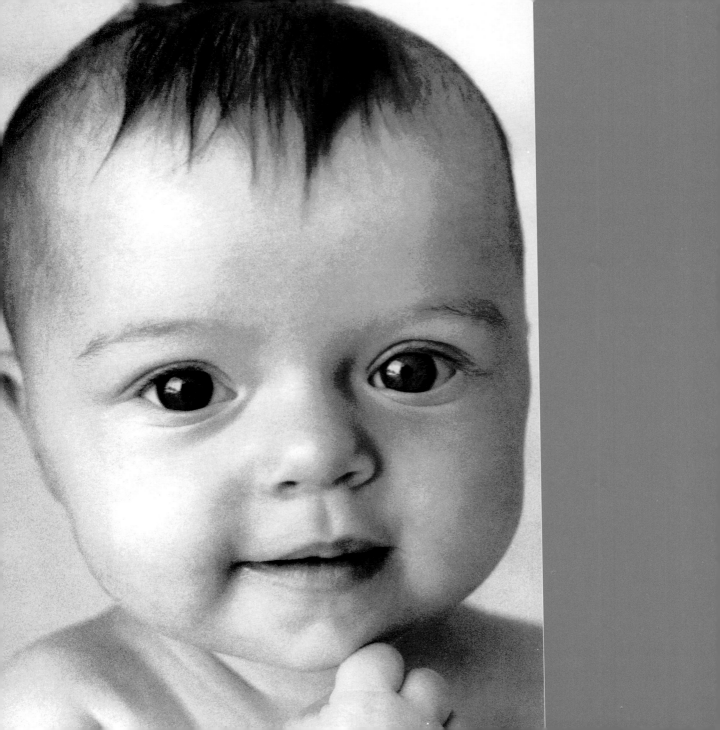

A LOVE LIKE NO OTHER

For more than twenty years, I have had the extraordinary privilege of being a personal coach to millions of people all over the world and from all walks of life.

My focus has always been to truly serve people by getting them in touch with their own unique gifts—to assist them in appreciating and utilizing their innate capacity to give, grow, learn, love, contribute, and become more than they are presently.

As the parent of four amazing young souls, I know there is nothing more important, challenging, or fulfilling than the love we have for our children. Parenting provides the ultimate challenge and the ultimate gift. It provides us with the leverage to make the most of ourselves, so we have more to give our children. Through parenting, we become teachers, protectors, providers, cheerleaders, disciplinarians, role models, and, often, students. By becoming the most outstanding parents we can possibly be, we can raise children to be gifts—gifts we give back to the Creator who gave us life and the world that shaped that life.

That's why I am so excited to introduce you to this book and to its extraordinary author, Loren Slocum. I have known Loren for many years now, and I can tell you that she is an extremely loving person whose commitment to growing and contributing is virtually unmatched.

Loren is not only an extraordinary mom and working mother, but a woman whose commitment to be her best propels her to new heights of joy and passion in both her family life and her business relationships.

This commitment has provided Loren with the drive to create books to help other mothers take their own first steps toward the success and happiness she is experiencing.

It is a privilege to write this foreword for such a dear friend. Loren's heart flows through this book, and the advice she offers may well help you to become the most outstanding mother you can be. Enjoy. And remember, *live*—and parent—*with passion!*

—Anthony Robbins

A WOMAN IS THE FULL CIRCLE. WITHIN HER IS THE POWER TO CREATE, NURTURE, AND TRANSFORM.

—Diane Mariechild

$\mathcal{B}$IRTH, n. *1. The gift of creation. 2. The ultimate reflection of God's creative power. 3. The beginning of a magical journey.*

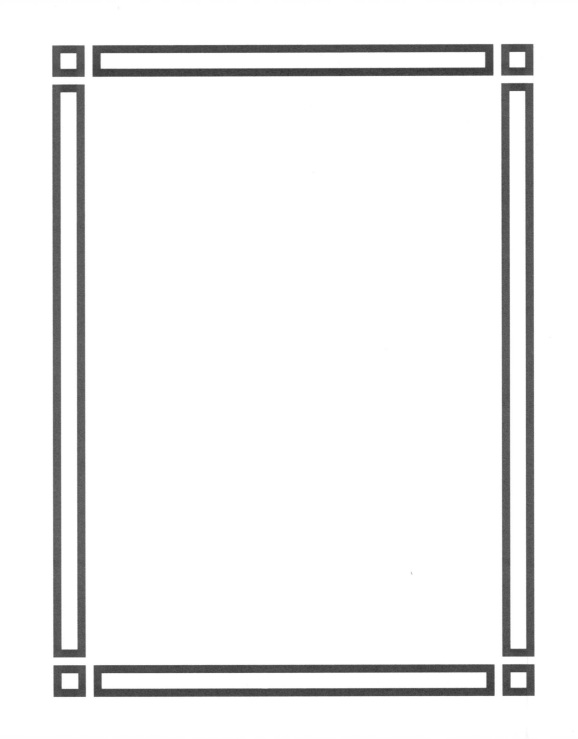

$\mathcal{D}$EAR READER,

This book is intended to celebrate you, your child, and the choice you have made to become an extraordinary mother. My highest hope is that by virtue of being a woman and a mother, you acknowledge what a wonderful example you have set for all your loved ones, but most importantly for your child.

I invite you to make this book your own by placing a favorite picture of you and your precious child here. Choose a photo that reflects a magical moment or special memory that you will keep in your heart forever. May it always remind you of the true unconditional love and wonder that surrounds motherhood.

*M*AKING THE DECISION TO HAVE A CHILD— IT'S MOMENTOUS. IT IS TO DECIDE FOREVER TO HAVE YOUR HEART GO WALKING AROUND OUTSIDE YOUR BODY.

—*Elizabeth Stone*

INTRODUCTION

What an incredible adventure writing this book has been for me! I feel as though I've just given birth again, and I want to thank you so much for allowing me to share my "delivery" with you. This book is the culmination of the most exhilarating, mind-bending, and profound journey I ever could have imagined. When I first learned I was pregnant, the initial excitement I experienced was mingled with more than just a little bit of fear. Already wholly committed to my career, my family, my friends, and a litany of community activities, I was worried about how I would possibly manage to balance everything. I knew that once my child was born, he would become the most important thing in the world to me, but I didn't want to live as though I were negotiating an obstacle course. I didn't want to have to give up anything or neglect any of the people or activities that were already so important to me. After some extensive soul-searching, a little good old-fashioned trial and error, and even a few tears, I finally came to the realization that I didn't have to sacrifice anything. I merely had to change my perspective and transform some of the beliefs that were keeping me from reaching my full potential. I had to develop a new attitude—*improvise, not compromise.*

Perhaps the greatest lesson I learned during this time—the lesson so many women desperately need to recognize in their lives—was the importance of acknowledging myself. As women, we do so much for other people—we nurture, support, soothe, comfort, console—we nourish the world. This role is an integral and wonderful part of being a woman! But, at times, we must learn to turn that energy inward and treat ourselves with the same level of caring we give others. We must embrace and celebrate the gifts we have been blessed with—use our resources to serve ourselves—so that we can build a better foundation to serve our children. In the midst of helping make everyone else's dreams come true, we often forget to acknowledge our own personal dreams, who we are inside, and what we really stand for in this world.

I have a little saying that reminds me of who I am. I encourage you to create one for yourself:

I'm a top-rated mama,
Leader extraordinare;
Taking care of all,
With elegance and flair.

Motherhood has truly enhanced my life and I am positive it has or will do the same for you, too. Do you remember when your parents told you, "You'll never know until you become a parent?" Well, now I know! Could you ever imagine experiencing a love so pure?

Although my son, Josua, is just over two years old, he has already traveled much of the United States, Canada, Europe, Fiji, and Australia. He has seen the Mona Lisa, been to the top of the Eiffel Tower, participated in a small Fijian village church mass, and heard the Sydney Symphony play in the world-renowned Opera House. Everywhere we go people are in awe of how content Josua is and how much he laughs; he is so open, bright, full of fun, light, and life. I take so much joy in seeing how many people love to be around him!

I am a mom who is committed to making myself, my family, my friends, and all my loved ones proud and happy, while simultaneously embracing the responsibility of raising an exuberant, healthy, balanced, and stimulated child. Whether you are fully aware of it or not, you, too, have those same responsibilities as a mom.

Being a parent can be the most rewarding and the most challenging experience of your life. Either way, you will grow! This book celebrates the joys of motherhood and is designed to make the transition into motherhood a rejuvenating learning experience. By honestly answering the questions presented in this book, you will set a standard for the mother you know you can be—the type of mother who sets an inspiring example for her child, her family, and for all others whose lives she touches.

You will notice this book is not a "how-to" book; it is something much more powerful. It is a "how to be" book. Our children learn from our example, from our lead, from our actions. We all know the phrase "It's not what you say, but what you do." The greatest gift you can give as a parent is to be someone your child admires, and respects.

That's my mom!

Be proud of who you are! Whether you are a first-time mom or a mom who has already experienced the joy of raising a precious little one, I hope that you realize what a powerful contribution you can make simply with your loving presence.

The beauty of the relationship between a mother and a child is what most inspired me to share these "baby basics" with moms all over the world. They are indeed the tools that can create a remarkable life and a compelling future for all of us.

—Loren

WE DO NO GREAT THINGS, ONLY SMALL THINGS WITH GREAT LOVE.

—*Mother Teresa*

EVERY DAY IS MOTHER'S DAY

A mother's incredible love, reassurance, and guidance gives
her child the strong foundation needed to confidently face any
obstacle that may arise. This foundation provides the safety
and support for a child to develop as an individual.
To celebrate Mother's Day every day, you must celebrate your
life and the life you've given to your family, to your community,
and to the world.

*C*ELEBRATION, n. *1. An everyday opportunity. 2. Gratitude with laughter. 3. Dancing to the beat of the heart. 4. A party that delights the soul. 5. Giving thanks for our blessings.*

Make Every Day Mother's Day

If you believe the greeting card companies and calendar makers, Mother's Day comes just once a year. But we know better! As moms, we know that Mother's Day has little to do with a special mark on a calendar. It's a state of mind—an awareness of the profound role we play in our children's lives each and every day.

Ralph Waldo Emerson once said, "Though we travel the world over to find the beautiful, we must carry it with us or we will find it not." As mothers, we are truly blessed, for we have our children as constant reminders of the beauty of life. With this in mind, our day-to-day activities take on a whole new significance. When you go to the market, you are not just shopping, you are providing nourishment for your loved ones—making simple grocery shopping a much more rewarding experience. When you clean the house, you are creating an environment of peace and order where joy and creativity can flourish unencumbered. When you run to the department store to purchase clothing for your family, you buy only resilient, quality wear—it has to protect your family from the elements! When you consistently take care of the necessities of life—your health, finances, career, home, and your own well-being—you are doing so with a greater purpose in mind. You are providing an example of how a person can truly live life with a sense of balance.

If you think being a mother is getting your children out of the house by the time they turn eighteen, then you're in for a long, struggle-filled haul! Being an amazing mother every day is an opportunity that has been offered to each of us. There is a saying—"live each day as if it were your last"—that translates into a belief I hold dear: "Being present in mind, body, and spirit during every precious moment of your life and the lives of others will guarantee a life lived with maximum joy and few regrets." Each of us is given the same twenty-four hours in a day. How and with whom we decide to spend those hours is totally up to us. As mothers, we make those choices for our children. The daily rituals we establish become the launching pad for the rest of their lives.

At times, we all feel a little off-kilter as mothers. For the most part, we learn by watching what others *do*. We allow what we feel and see to create an "I'm not doing anything right" syndrome because we compare ourselves and our lifestyles to those of other mothers whose lives or lifestyles may not in any way resemble our own. We forget that each situation is different and there are many choices and different styles of mothering. What we all should have in common is a strong belief that we are going to be amazing moms, in our own right, and do our best to lovingly handle anything that comes our way.

The cause of the "I'm not doing anything right" syndrome may be that we have not provided a strong enough foundation for *ourselves*. Building and strengthening our confidence and self-worth forms a sturdy base from which we can perform consistently and remind ourselves of the most important areas of our life. Those areas are the priorities that truly shape the emotional foundation of our daily lives.

It is only through our own awakening, our mindful connection with the essence of who we are—givers of life, custodians of the soul—that we can impart true wisdom to our children and make every day a celebration of motherhood.

Be an Extraordinary Mom

Being an extraordinary mother is not about going through the motions—feeding, bathing, changing, dressing—it's about true and loving connection between you and your child every day; it's about being a steward of your child's joyful development. Being an extraordinary mom is not *what you do*, it's about *who you are*.

Imagine your child as the adult you would like him or her to become—happy, loving, conscious, kind, giving, strong, wise. Imagine the kind of mother who would raise a child of that caliber. Now is the time to "be" that mother. . . .

*E*VERY
CHILD IS OUR
OPPORTUNITY
TO SHAPE THE
FUTURE OF
THE WORLD.
—*Loren Slocum*

*M*OTHERHOOD, n. *1. The origin of life.*
2. The shepherding of hope. 3. The teaching of love.
4. An example of selflessness. 5. A chance to positively change the world.

*T*O BE A PERSON YOU'RE NOT IS TO WASTE THE PERSON YOU ARE.

—*Anonymous*

Be Yourself

We welcome the birth of our children with great celebration, and with good reason!
But equally deserving of celebration is the birth of our own motherhood. With this
new chapter of life comes the acknowledgment of the unconditional love and
support we will provide for our child the minute we find out another person is going
to become a part of our lives (either through pregnancy or adoption). You often
hear people say, "they broke the mold when she was born." Well, guess what? They
did! You are a unique woman and a special mother in many ways. As one of my
dear friends always says, "God bless you for being you!" Celebrate you!

One of the most important qualities of motherhood is just being yourself. It is
obvious to everyone (yourself, your child, and others) when you are being your true
self; it is just as obvious when you are being fake or acting like someone you're not.
Being yourself doesn't mean you shouldn't strive to be better; it doesn't mean you
should stop learning or asking for help. Being yourself means that when you get
advice or learn something new, you integrate the parts of what you learned into
what already works for you and add your own flair to it. During your parenting
journey you're going to hear all sorts of advice. Remember, there is more than one
way to parent (thankfully!). So develop your own style. Take the best of who you
are and let that be the foundation of your parenting style. Don't change who you
are. Continue to be you and all the other "skills" will fall into place. As your child
grows, you will grow too. That is the beauty of motherhood . . . and of life.

*L*ET NO MAN BE DELUDED THAT A
KNOWLEDGE OF THE PATH CAN SUBSTITUTE FOR
PUTTING ONE FOOT IN FRONT OF THE OTHER.

—*Mary Caroline Richards*

Be Wise

Wisdom comes from within; looking internally is the best way to solve external challenges. We all possess, deep within ourselves, the knowledge and wisdom to do what is right. God only gives us the challenges he knows we can handle. We intuitively know the correct path to take if we just pause a moment in our hurried lives to focus our minds and trust the answers that come to us. The people to admire most are those who take a deep breath before they make a decision, who use calm conviction to move forward with love and compassion, rather than those who get swallowed up by the emotion of the moment.

As mothers, we must trust the wisdom God has blessed us with in order to make decisions for ourselves and our children—decisions that feel right. Remember, the decisions you make may not always achieve your desired result, but no decision is wrong if you choose to learn something from it. What an extraordinary role model you will be for your child, if you approach life with this type of attitude. Your child will see a mother willing to make mistakes, but not willing to give up! Adopting a calm, determined, and sometimes daring approach to life is an excellent lesson for your children and possibly the wisest step you will ever take for yourself.

$\mathcal{E}$VERY WOMAN
SHOULD REMEMBER
THAT WE HAVE THE
INTUITIVE RADAR TO
KNOW EXACTLY HOW
TO LISTEN TO OUR
CHILDREN, WHAT TO
SAY TO OUR CHILDREN,
AND HOW TO LOVE
OUR CHILDREN. . . .
WE LEARN WHAT THEY
WANT, WE LEARN
WHAT THEY NEED,
BY LISTENING TO
THEM AND WATCHING
THEM. THEY KNOW, AND
THEY WILL TELL US.
—*Marianne Williamson*

Be Understanding

Being understanding means being compassionate, open, intuitive, and present (in mind and body). The first step toward understanding is truly listening—with your heart. Remember, hearing is not the same as listening. You can hear someone's voice, but are you really listening to his or her message?

With the amount of challenges and activities that life provides us, it can often be easier to react than to try to understand what is going on with our children. When your child is first born you hone these listening skills—your baby cannot utter a word and yet you innately know when he is hungry, tired, or uncomfortable just by the way he cries or fusses. Keep these same listening skills with you even when your children can talk; try to understand how they are feeling, not just what they are saying. This level of caring will transform your relationship with your child. It will help you avoid conflict, build trust, and strengthen the special bond between the two of you.

REFLECTIONS . . .
AN ESSENTIAL TOOL FOR MOTHERHOOD

Reflection is often achieved through asking questions of yourself.
Asking quality questions means that you will get quality answers.
This, in turn, will take you directly to the heart of the matter,
to what is most important for you to learn. Reflection means taking
the time to search and discover new ways to improve yourself,
your child, and being a mother.

$\mathcal{T}$HE PRESENT, n. 1. *The moment when you open your eyes. 2. A timeless second. 3. A state of being in the moment. 4. When you move from your head to your heart. 5. The determination of your future. 6. A precious gift.*

Ask Quality Questions

As moms, we have an awesome responsibility and privilege: We truly mold the leaders of the next generation. The first human contact our babies have is with us. Through our touch, they learn love, caring, tenderness, safety, and strength. And as our babies become more fully a part of the world, they learn by observing the example we set. Our actions make a much bigger impression than our words, so it is important for us always to act in the best, most positive manner.

A valuable tool that allows me to act positively on a daily basis, rather than settle for my second best, is to ask myself quality questions. Specifically, I ask myself the "Mommy Morning Questions," the "Mommy Evening Questions," and the "Mommy Problem-Solving Questions." How powerful are these questions? Quite simply, they can change your life. No matter how heavy the demands are on your time and energy, just taking a moment or two to reflect on these questions can move you instantly from feeling overwhelmed and exhausted to being excited, grateful, passionate, and energized. We experience everything through our own filters of the world. Something that seems terrible or tragic to one person may be incredible and uplifting to another. These questions are designed to assist you in creating better filters for yourself, so you get more out of each day, each situation, and each precious moment.

You may think you do not have the time to answer such questions, but you must commit to make the time. Just as you make time for other things that are truly important—like feeding your baby, changing your baby's diaper, or giving your baby a bath—above all, you must make time to raise an exceptional child. Quality questions can be a powerful tool to help you do just that. These questions have been lifesavers for me in all sorts of situations, and I know they can be the same for anyone else who has too much to do and too little time—in short, for anyone who is a mom!

CLEVER PEOPLE SEEM NOT TO FEEL THE
NATURAL PLEASURE OF BEWILDERMENT,
AND ARE ALWAYS ANSWERING QUESTIONS
WHEN THE CHIEF RELISH OF A LIFE
IS TO GO ON ASKING THEM.

—*Frank Moore Colby, "Simple Simon,"* The Colby Essays

KEYS TO ASKING QUESTIONS AND HAVING THEM WORK:

- YOU MUST ASK EACH QUESTION UNTIL YOU COME UP WITH THE ANSWER THAT IS RIGHT FOR YOU. If you ask a question like, "What is my child going to teach me today?" then focus on how this answer can make a positive difference in your child's day and, ultimately, his life.

- YOU MUST TAKE A MOMENT TO SEARCH YOUR HEART FOR EACH ANSWER. Once you come up with the right answer, take a deep breath in and acknowledge its potential impact.

- ASK THESE QUESTIONS CONSISTENTLY. The more you ask the questions, the better you will be at finding meaningful answers that come from your heart. I ask these questions a minimum of once a day. I come up with answers quickly because I have conditioned myself through repetition. You will find that the answers become more and more profound each day. Also, by making the question-asking process a habit, you will start to notice that you automatically ask them at other times during your day. I can't tell you how many times I have had problems arise, where I am immediately able to ask myself a "Mommy Problem-Solving Question" and the answer helps me transcend that problem.

- READ THE QUESTIONS AND GET IN THE HABIT OF USING THEM. Put them on little cards you see every day. Put the "Mommy Morning Questions" on your bathroom mirror, the "Mommy Evening Questions" on your nightstand, and the "Mommy Problem-Solving Questions" in your purse. The next time a challenging situation arises and you find yourself getting panicky or "losing it," just stop, take a few deep breaths, start asking yourself these great questions, and focus on all the wonderful answers you devise. I guarantee these question/answer sessions will make a huge difference in the way you react. Why is that important? *Because little eyes are always watching.*

Mommy Morning

QUESTIONS

How can my child and I
experience our love in an
extraordinary new way today?

This set of questions is designed to help you start your day in the best possible place emotionally for you and your child, and to assist you in focusing on what will really make a difference in your and your child's life. By asking yourself these questions every morning, you will uncover opportunities for learning, growth, love, patience, happiness, and many other powerful emotions that often are overlooked in the daily life of a busy mom.

Teaching/Learning

What is my baby going to teach me today?

What am I going to teach my baby today?

What can I do today to help my child learn and grow?

What can I do today to learn and grow?

How can I be a role model for my baby today?

Connection & Love

In the midst of my busy day, how can I still remain grateful?

How can I be even more patient today?

Who do I love?

Who loves me?

How can I show my love even more?

Fun & Laughter

What am I most excited about today?

What am I most proud of in my life today?

What am I most grateful for in my life today?

How can I create even more special moments for my family and myself?

How can I take care of my family and myself even better?

What is something special that I can do for my baby and myself today?

Who is my child going to become because of me today?

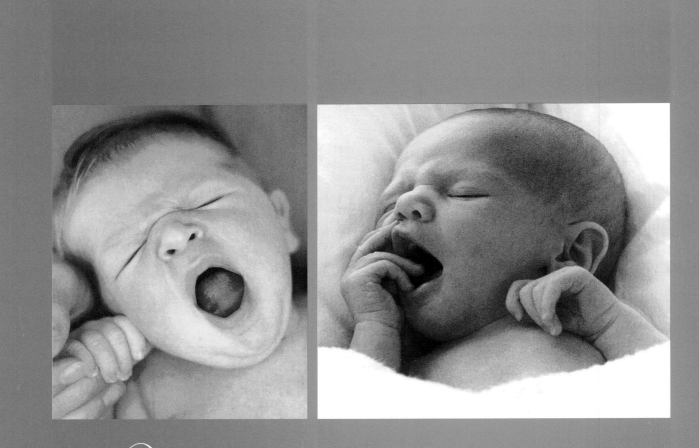

$\mathcal{O}$THER PEOPLE IN MY LIFE HAVE HELPED MY SOUL TO SING A SONG. . . . YOU, MY CHILD, HAVE CAUSED MY HEART TO SING A SYMPHONY.

—*Donna Ringo*

MOMMY EVENING QUESTIONS

What did my child and I learn
from each other today?

This set of questions is your greatest teacher. The way we become better at something is by looking at how we are doing along the way. These questions give you a chance to increase your awareness of how you are connecting with your child: Where are the gaps in your child's growth, in your growth as a family, in your becoming the best mom you can be? Remind yourself that you will rarely, if ever, be perfect, but the most profound growth will come from your pursuit of being the best mom you can be. The key is to become just a tiny bit better every day. This is where the greatest rewards are hidden.

SELF-CARE

Did I pause and breathe today?

How did I take care of myself physically today?

Did I balance what I needed to do with what I wanted to accomplish today?

FUN & LAUGHTER

What did my baby do to make me laugh?

What did I do to make my baby laugh?

CONNECTION & LOVE

What did my baby and I do together today?

How many times did my baby hear me say, "I love you"?

Teaching

What word did I teach my baby today?

How did I see things from my baby's perspective?

Did I read to my baby today?

Reflection

What made me smile today?

What made me proud today?

How was I a great mom today?

Important versus urgent

What worked today?

Did I focus on what was truly important today?

Was I happy at least 90 percent of the time today?

How could I be even happier tomorrow?

Mommy

PROBLEM-SOLVING

QUESTIONS

What would an extraordinary mom
do in this situation?

As a mother, you will be tested again and again—perhaps more than in any other role you perform in life! There will be tests of patience, love, perseverance, endurance, selflessness, caring, maturity, compassion, and discipline—more tests than you could ever imagine before actually becoming a mom. How you respond to these tests will provide your moments of greatest growth, learning, and teaching. These questions will offer you a helping hand in facing the never-ending challenges of being a busy mom. They will assist you in focusing on getting through a situation and, more important, on becoming a better mom—strengthening you and, in turn, your child, with the resolution of each situation.

What would an extraordinary mom do in this situation?

How am I going to grow as a result of this challenge?

How will this moment serve me, my baby, and my family?

How is my baby going to become a better adult because of the way I handle this experience?

How can I find more patience, love, strength, or resourcefulness right now?

If a child is to keep alive his inborn sense of wonder, he needs the companionship of at least one adult who can share it, rediscovering with him the joy, excitement and mystery of the world we live in.

—*Rachel Carson,* The Sense of Wonder

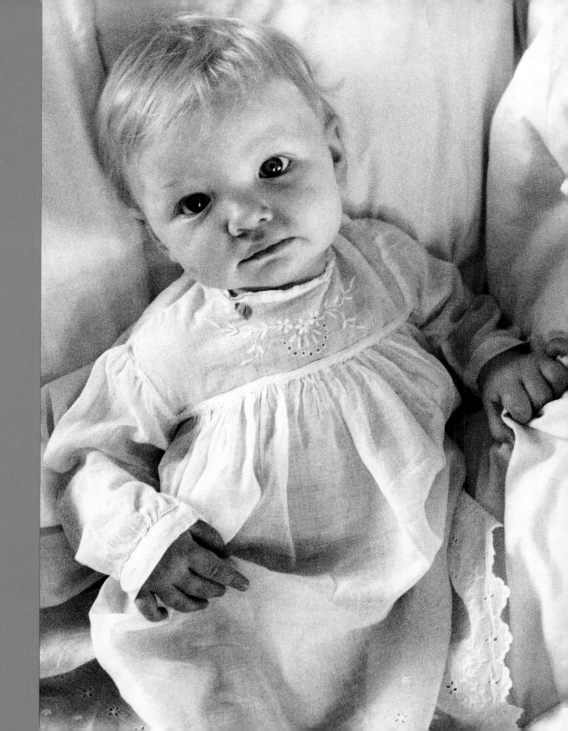

CHILD, n. 1. *A gift from God to be handled with care.*
2. *An open path of love. 3. True innocence. 4. Hope for a better world.*

No Greater Love Means . . .

*T*O LOVE AND TO BE LOVED IS TO FEEL THE SUN FROM BOTH SIDES.

—*David Viscott*

Truly Loving My Child

Truly loving my little one means making sure that he has all the things he needs, not just the basics of clothing, food, shelter, and warmth, but also the intangibles like values, morals, confidence, standards, and, most important, love. Love is the foundation for creating anything of meaning in life, especially when raising a child. Working from a strong foundation of love, all things seem possible because we feel a sense of glorious abundance flowing through us. We seem to have more to give than we ever thought possible. A love so full, so complete creates a unique bond between mother and child—a love that only grows stronger with each new experience. Cherish this level of love and take the time to communicate that affection to him through your touch, your patience, your understanding, and your actions. This level of intimacy will allow you and your baby to appreciate and experience the world more profoundly.

LOVING MOM

Mom always takes time to show me and tell me
she loves me. I can see Mom's love for me in
her eyes. I can feel her love in every little touch.
I can hear the love in her beautiful voice. I have
the most loving mom in the world!

BEING CURIOUS WITH MY CHILD

Children look at the world in the most innocent and curious way—their eyes full of wonder and awe. Having a child offers us the opportunity to rediscover the wonders of the world. If you are looking for a new perspective on life, kneel down beside your baby and take a look at the world from her vantage point. Go ahead . . . get down on the floor and try to comprehend the thoughts that must be racing through your baby's mind as she delicately twists each fiber of your plush carpeting or tries to nibble her own little toes. There are so many ways to encourage your baby to make new discoveries. Exploring the world, hand in hand, makes life a bright package just waiting to be opened.

ADVENTURE MOM

My mom is always showing me that life is an
adventure. Looking at each and every experience
as a chance to discover—discover the unknown,
discover the possibilities. Sometimes, adventures
can be scary (like learning to walk, falling off
my bed, or learning to ice skate) but my mom
makes sure I celebrate each of these opportunities.
She reminds me that these experiences help me
to joyfully anticipate future adventures—some I will
share with her and some I will discover on my own.

$\mathcal{S}$TART TODAY AS A CHILD DOES, FULL OF
LIGHT AND THE CLEAREST VISION.

—*Brenda Veland*

BEING PRESENT WITH MY CHILD

When you're feeding, bathing, and playing with your baby, are you giving him your full attention? Your undivided attention is exactly what "being present" with your child means. Each moment you spend together is a gift that allows you to connect with your little one on a more intimate level. The first key to being present is to listen, not just with your ears, but with your heart. Look for the real meaning in your baby's communication. By learning to understand your child's subtle messages you will strengthen the tremendous bond between the two of you. The second key to being present is to see, not only with your eyes, but with your soul. A mother's intuition is often a clearer window to her child's soul than the naked eye. Choose to be present with your baby in mind, body, and spirit—giving your whole self each moment you spend with your little angel will add incredible joy and fulfillment to motherhood.

 PRESENT MOM

When my mommy and I are together, she gives me her full attention. She understands what I need and want even though I can't talk as well as she can. The biggest gift my mommy gives me is just spending time with me. She is definitely a "present" mom!

PLAYING WITH MY CHILD

How lucky you are! You finally have a perfectly adorable little excuse to be a kid again—to play silly games and make funny faces, to build sand castles on the beach, to swing on the swing set, and to test out all the possible toys your child might desire. Playing with your child may just be the easiest part of motherhood, or at least the most fun. So what does it truly entail? Time—a hot commodity in today's hustle-bustle world—and imagination. Be creative and be generous, because time spent playing with your child is the most precious time of all—for both of you.

Who can make the funniest face?

How many tickle spots can you find?

Who can hop like a bunny rabbit? "Ribbit" like a frog?

What amazing adventure will the two of you take?
(A trip to the store or reading a story.)

PLAYFUL MOM

My mom and I play in lots of different ways.
One way is that my mom shares some of her special
treasures with me. Mommy loves watching me
discover the beauty of the simplest gifts that some
grown-ups take for granted. What means the most
to me is when my mommy says I remind her to stop
and celebrate life every chance she can! I'm happy
when everything my mom does is play to her!

*I*T IS THE
WISE MOTHER
THAT GIVES
HER CHILD ROOTS
AND WINGS.

—*Chinese Proverb*

SHOWING MY CHILD WHAT IS POSSIBLE

How many times do we impose limits on those we love without ever realizing what we are doing? The purpose of the fences we put up is, more often than not, to keep those we care about from getting hurt. It is our job to protect our children and to make sure they follow the "right path." Finding the "right path" is a difficult task—a path that leads one child to their promised land may lead another child astray. Let your children take risks. Let them find their calling. Let them experience what their hearts tell them to experience. One of the best ways you can help them find their paths is by following your own calling, fulfilling your special purpose on this earth. Expose your child to as many different experiences as you can. Take them to places you love, and to places you wouldn't go to on your own in a million years—an art museum or a war memorial, a ceramics class or a woodworking shop, the beach or the mountains. Go to a classical music concert. Eat at a Greek tavern. The way your children will know what lies ahead in this great big world is if you take the time to show them all the wonderful gifts available. You know what else might happen? You might enjoy all the new experiences yourself! Remember, don't "freak out" if your child tries something and fails or doesn't enjoy it. To teach your children what is possible, you must allow them to fail and, more important, to succeed through their own discoveries. With supervised self-discovery, you will help them learn and grow as individuals.

EXAMPLE MOM

Mom never lets other people's limits stop her from being the best in the whole wide world. My mom shows me what is good and honest and true not only by telling me but by showing me with her actions. She is truly an example of what is possible if you really believe.

When I grow up, I want to be just like her.

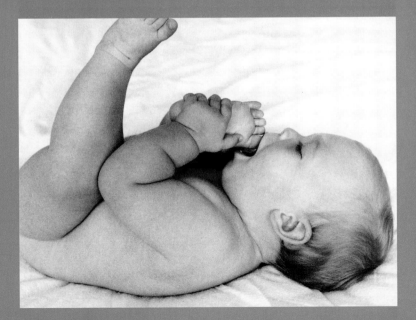

TEACHING AND LEARNING WITH MY CHILD

There is so much to be learned and experienced from life, it is hard to know where to begin. Even as you lead the way, your child teaches you in turn. Through our children, we see the world with new vision, hear life in different harmonies, and feel textures through the hands of a fresh new soul. This new reaction to the world is an important reminder that one of the primary roles of motherhood is to teach. During your teaching, you will often find the roles reversed, as though God sent you your child to be your teacher. At different moments, you will sit in awe as your child discovers something so simple yet so new—and through her wonder, you will be transformed.

Learning will come through ways you never imagined or planned. Sometimes the lessons shared by you and your child will come in your wildest moments together. You cannot plan everything you want to occur in order to teach your child the lessons of life. My son's godmother once said, "If you want to make God laugh, tell him your plan." In other words, realize that as many things as there are that you want to teach your child, there are equally as many for you to learn. Be grateful for the opportunity to learn from the honest innocence of your child's soul.

TEACHER MOM

Mom always wants me to find the best, deep
inside. She helps me to walk, talk, learn, and laugh.
She shows me new things like animals, sand castles,
puddles, and rainbows and explains them to me.
She always looks for the good I have inside and
then helps me express it to the world.

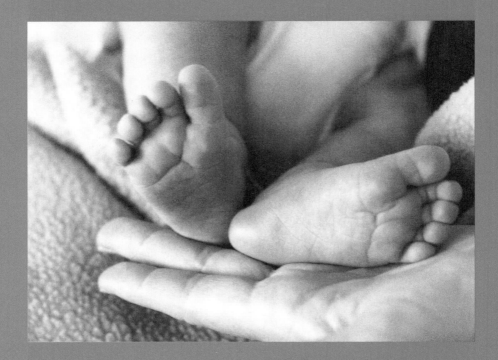

*L*ORD OF THE LOVING HEART, MAY MINE
BE LOVING TOO. LORD OF THE GENTLE HANDS,
MAY MINE BE GENTLE TOO. LORD OF THE WILLING
FEET, MAY MINE BE WILLING TOO. SO I MAY GROW
MORE LIKE THEE IN ALL I SAY AND DO.

—*Phyllis Garlick*

Having Gratitude and Faith

Give thanks that you have been blessed with a wonderful baby. Motherhood is an unparalleled privilege. Your duty is to love your baby no matter who or what he or she becomes. Never compare your baby to others. Your baby may have physical or mental limitations, but you must believe that those extra challenges were given to your family for a reason. Believe that God thought you were one of the few people who could handle such a challenge and that is why you were given such a special child.

I believe that God chooses your baby and your baby's personality to help you become the best person you can possibly be. Have faith that you will be guided to make the choices that allow you and your child to grow. There is not a moment that goes by that I am not humbly grateful for being chosen to be a mom. Being a mother is an honor and a challenge—a tiny fragment of the future is molded by our hands. I hope you, too, have these incomparable feelings. If we, as mothers, commit to raise better children, I honestly believe we can heal the world one soul at a time.

ANGEL MOM

To me, my mom is an angel. She is so pure and so special. Her eyes reach souls. Her touch mends hearts. She is sweet yet strong, simple yet elegant. Sometimes, if I really concentrate, I can see the glow of the halo above her head. My mom is truly the loveliest woman you will ever behold.

YOU MUST BE THE CHANGE YOU WISH
TO SEE IN THE WORLD.

—*Gandhi*

START TODAY

We as mothers have been entrusted to provide a physical and
emotional environment that nurtures, teaches, and inspires
our children. As we stand on the threshold of a new millennium,
a time of unforeseen challenge and opportunity, it is imperative
that we rise to our gift of being mothers.

Commit to a life that continues to make love the number-one
priority and a life where you truly cherish each moment.

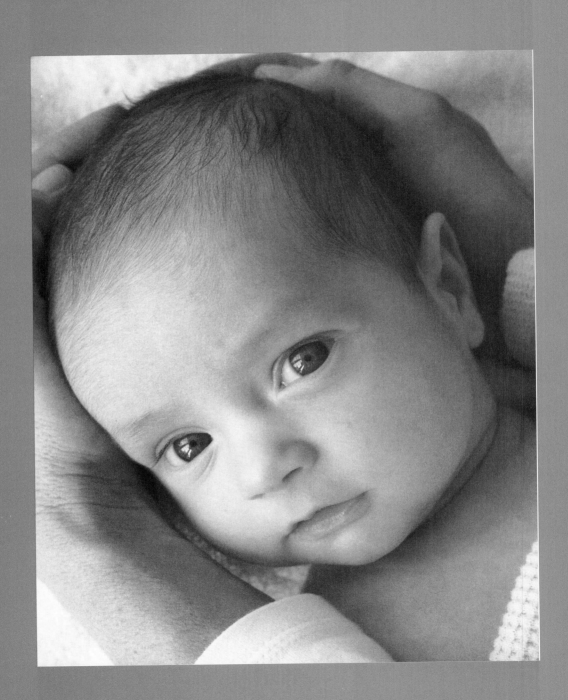

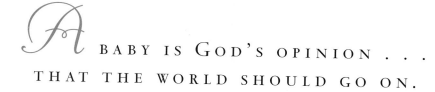

A BABY IS GOD'S OPINION . . .
THAT THE WORLD SHOULD GO ON.

—Carl Sandburg

$\mathcal{T}$HE FUTURE, n. *1. A reward for being active in the present. 2. A place of curiosity. 3. Fast paced. 4. Your choice!*

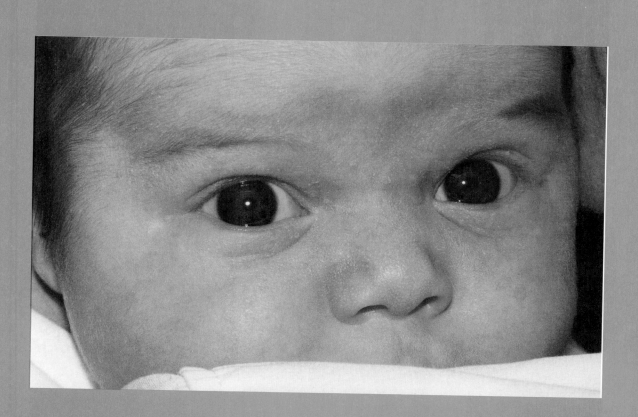

ABOUT THE AUTHOR

LOREN SLOCUM: mother, author, speaker, mentor

Loren Slocum's *No Greater Love* illustrates her passion for life, as witnessed by thousands of women and men throughout the world. It is this passion that keeps her vibrant and young, and magnifies her extraordinary relationships with her family and her career.

For the past eight years, as the crew director for the Anthony Robbins Companies, Loren has been responsible for the training and event management of thousands of volunteers worldwide. Loren also leads the marketing department as vice president for Momentus Productions, which serves nonprofit organizations.

The mother of three-year-old Josua Owen Slocum, Loren firmly believes, "It is who you are being in everyday life that makes you a great mom." This core belief about motherhood has been fueled by her relationship with Shore Slocum. She lives in Portland, Oregon.

For more information on attending one of Loren Slocum's special engagements, or to order the *No Greater Love* CD or any of her other products, please call 877-659-MOMS. (Photos: 48, 82)

COLLEEN FUTCH MORGANS: lead photographer

Colleen Morgans has been photographing children all of her adult life. She began her career photographing the children she looked after while working as a nanny in college. Soon she had a booming business in Southern California taking black-and-white, natural pictures of children in their own homes. Colleen and her husband, Lance, have an eighteen-month-old little girl, Lily Grace, and are expecting their second child at the end of the year.

KELLY GIEZENTANNER: Cover photo and photos on pages vi, viii, xxvii, 34, 46, 64, and 84. Kelly has been specializing in fine children's portraits for six years. She owns Hopscotch Gallery and resides in Asheville, North Carolina.

PHOTO: p. 78, Michael Segal